Terms of Use &

Credits

All fonts, clipart, and photographs were obtained through Canva Pro.

This resource was reviewed by a variety of neurodivergent individuals & neurodiversity affirming professionals.

THANK YOU SO MUCH TO ALL INVOLVED:

- Mary Bennett
- Gale
- Emily Starling
- Grace Brandon
- Sarah Weber
- Elizabeth Hepler
- Nikki Fries
- Lauren Greenlief

Dedication

This book is dedicated to my past, present, and future students and clients. All neurodivergent individuals deserve to feel safe, comfortable, and authentic at school, home, and in the community.

contents

introduction

Objectives:

- Assess current knowledge
- Define key terminology
- Compare & contrast neurotypes
- Research neurodivergent celebrities

What I Know Already

Answer the questions below about what you already know regarding neurodiversity.

	Not so much 👎	Kind of ✊	Definitely 👍
I know what the term neurodiversity means			
I know and can describe different neurotypes			
I know about my own neurotype			
I can name different communication styles			
I understand and utilize self-advocacy			
I understand the term multiple perspectives			
I know steps to solve problems			
I can identify what I look for in a friend or relationship			

What is Neurodiversity?

Neurodiversity refers to brain differences in learning, listening, communicating, socializing, and thinking. We can call the different brains, neurotypes.

Neurodivergent brains work differently than how science expects the brain to work. Examples include:

Autism	ADHD	Dyslexia	Dyscalculia
Tourette's	Bipolar	Depression	Anxiety
Obsessive-Compulsive Disorder	Oppositional Defiant Disorder	Sensory Processing	Developmental Delay
Specific Learning Disability	Gifted	Dissociative Identity Disorder	Epilepsy

Why do Neurotypes Matter?

Different brains need different supports. Some brains need silence while others need noise. Some need to fidget while others need to sit still. Some like eye contact and some hate it. There is no right way to learn, listen, communicate, socialize, think, etc.

Why is it important to know about neurodiversity?

_____

_____

_____

What are 3 things that may differ between neurotypes?

_____

_____

_____

Neurodivergent Celebrities

Emma Watson (ADHD)
Actress known for her role as Hermoine Granger in Harry Potter.

Octavia Spencer (Dyslexia)
Actress known for The Help, Hidden Figures, and The Shape of Water.

Lewis Capaldi (Tourette's)
Scottish singer-songwriter.

Tim Burton (Autism)
Fantasy and horror director and animator.

Do you know any other neurodivergent celebrities?

Neurodivergent Celebrity

Use Google, social media, books, etc. to research another neurodivergent person. It could be an actor, scientist, gamer, influencer, historical figure, etc.

Name:_____

Neurotype: _____

Claim to fame:_____

3 fun facts about this person:

1._____

_____

2. _____

_____

3. _____

_____

me & my brain

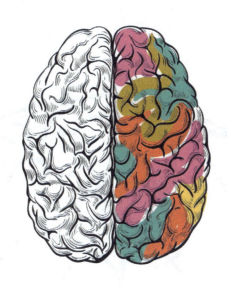

Objectives:

- Reflect on own brain and interests
- Identify accommodations
- Identify strengths
- Identify needs

Me & My Brain

Everyone's brain thinks, feels, and processes information differently. This means we all find different things interesting or important. Decorate the brain below to demonstrate what is important to you. You can draw, write, etc.

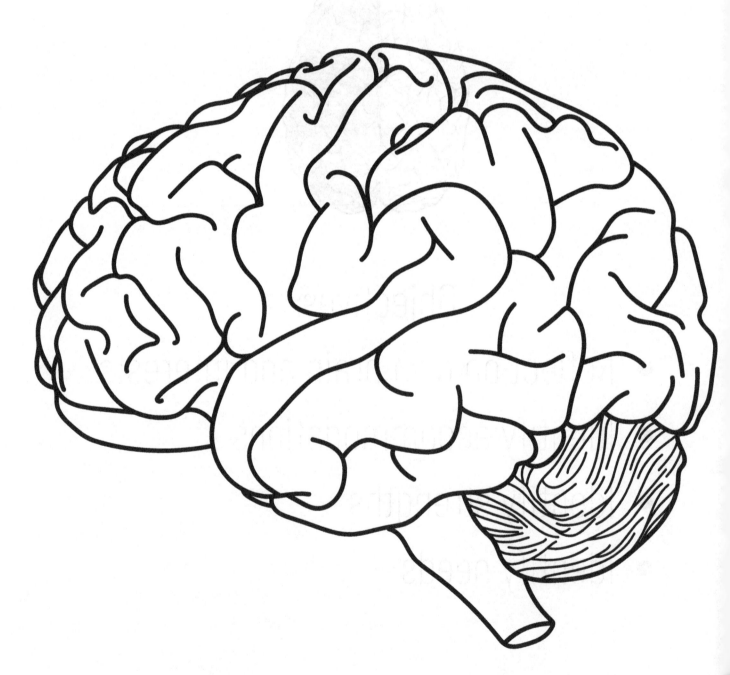

I'm Neurodivergent... So What?!

What's your neurotype?

_____

Knowing your neurotype can help you understand how your brain works. It is important to understand how you learn best, what supports you may need, your communication and social style, etc.

Do some research! Use Google, articles, books, social media, etc. to find 3 characteristics of your neurotype that you relate to:

1. _____

2. _____

3. _____

My Accommodations

All neurotypes need tools and strategies to learn. However, no two people learn in the exact same way. Pick the strategies or tools that help you learn best. These are accommodations.

Sitting still	Movement	Fidgets
Music	Silence	Talking
Repetition	Breaking it down	Looking at the teacher
Looking away from teacher	Using a computer	Writing with pen and paper
Sitting in a chair	Sitting on the floor	Standing
Taking breaks	Talking about the topic	Reading about the topic
Listening to a lecture	Something different: _____ _____	

My Brain is not Broken!

Sometimes environments or situations may be harder to navigate because of our brain's differences.
Name 3 things you may need accommodations for:

1. _____

2. _____

3. _____

HOWEVER, just because some things may be more difficult, doesn't mean your brain needs to be fixed. Your neurotype has strengths, too. Name 5 strengths you have:

1. _____

2. _____

3. _____

4. _____

5. _____

communication

Objectives:

- Define & identify communication styles
- Define & identify communication modalities
- Define & identify communication intents
- Define & identify effective communication

Different Brain, Different Communication

Different neurotypes communicate in different ways. There are many styles of communication. We may use more than one style.

Direct Communication: saying exactly what you mean

what you mean ●- - - - - - - - -→ what you say

Indirect Communication: talking around what you mean

what you mean ⌇ what you say

Nonverbal Communication: the way your body, face, gestures, volume, and tone of voice communicates

Direct Communication
saying exactly what you mean

Assertive: expressing your point of view in a way that is clear and direct. "I didn't like when you did that because..."

Aggressive: using demanding, controlling language. "Never do that to me again, or else."

Blunt: being honest, no matter how others feel. "That was really stupid to do."

Info-dumping: making preferred interests clear by talking about the topic in detail. "...and there's about 700 types of dinosaurs including..."

Indirect Communication
talking around what you mean.

Sarcastic: saying words that mean the opposite of your true meaning to show frustration, insult someone, or to use humor. "Oh, I really LOVED when you did that..."

Passive: avoiding saying what we want or need. "Yeah it was fine that you said that, I didn't mind" (even if you DID mind).

Small-talk: using niceties and routine phrases. "How about the weather this week...?"

Style 101

Look at each picture. What communication style/s do you think are being used? Why?

It's really nice today. I'm glad the sun is out!

_____

_____

_____

_____

_____

_____

_____

_____

Superheroes LOVE eating rice!

... and there's Dalmatians, Bulldogs, Labs...

_____

_____

_____

_____

Set the Style Scene

Reflect on each communication style. When might you or another person use these styles?

Assertive: _____
_____

Aggressive: _____
_____

Indirect: _____
_____

Sarcasm: _____
_____

Info-dumping: _____
_____

Blunt: _____
_____

My Communication

Knowing our communication style can help us communicate clearly, repair breakdowns, and advocate for ourselves.

What type/s of communication do you use most often?

_____

What type/s of communication do you think are harder to understand?

_____

What could you say to educate a communication partner about your communication style?

_____

_____

_____

_____

Respect All Modalities

Not only are there different communication styles, but there are also different ways to communicate. We call these modalities.

Language based: this includes spoken language, written language, sign language, & AAC.

Nonverbal based: this includes communication done by our body, face, hands, tone, etc.

Language Modalities

Some modalities utilize specific words, grammar, and other aspects of language. These modalities include:

Spoken: using our mouths to say words. Also known as mouth words.

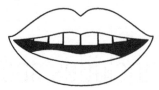

Written: using spelling and writing tools to communicate. This includes physically writing, typing, texting, email, social media, DMing, and more.

AAC: the use of technology to communicate (pictures, tablet, text to speech, etc.)

Sign Language: a language system using hand movements and placements to represent vocabulary, grammar, and meaning. Most often used by Deaf/deaf individuals.

Nonverbal Modalities

Some modalities don't use words at all.
These modalities include:

Gestures: using body movements, especially the hands or head, to communicate a message

Body Language: the way your body communicates messages. This includes turning away, slumping shoulders, crossing arms, etc.

Facial Expressions: the way your mouth, eyes, eyebrows, etc. move to express yourself

Tone of Voice: how you sound when you say your message. This can include volume and inflection.

Modalities in the Moment

Reflect on each communication modality. When might you or another person use these modalities?

Spoken: _____

_____

Written: _____

_____

Gestures: _____

_____

Body Language: _____

_____

Facial Expressions: _____

_____

AAC: _____

_____

Now, About the WHY

When we communicate, it helps to think about WHY we are communicating. These are called communication intents.

For example, this group of friends may be communicating to say hello, catch up about their weekends, or be meeting for the first time.

Misunderstandings, or communication breakdowns, can happen if our intent and style don't match.

Intents

Here are *some* of the intents we may use:

Socializing

- Greet
- Pretend
- Gossip
- Humor
- Gain attention
- Plan
- Tell stories
- Share interests
- Comment
- Ask/Answer
- Compliment
- Flirt

Learning

- Answer
- Ask
- Report
- Comment/describe
- Remind
- Clarify
- Tell stories/events

Protesting

- Ask to stop
- Express dislikes
- Disagree
- Negotiate
- Argue
- Complain
- Give directions

Advocating

- Ask for help
- Regulate
- Report
- Describe pain and illness
- Remind
- Clarify
- Express discomfort or dislike

My Intents

Which intents do you communicate most frequently?

request	protest	attention	telling stores
clarify messages	express interests	flirt	use humor
complain	comment	ask	describe
advocate	regulate	socialize	direct people
gossip	disagree	compliment	remind others
pretend	agree	negotiate	argue
answer	report something	express dislike or discomfort	Other: _____ _____

Are there intents you wish you used more frequently?

_____

_____

_____

Effective Communication

Only YOU can decide if your communication was effective. Effective communication gets us what we wanted or needed from the interaction. Your communication is NOT dependent on neurotypical social norms like eye contact. It only depends on your own opinion!

Effective communication can look and sound different for everyone. Each picture above shows different types of communication and interactions.

Step To It

	Action	Questions to ask myself
	Pick intended message	What am I trying to communicate? What do I want? How do I want the other person to feel? What's my intent?
	Plan it out	Will I use spoken words, facial expressions, written words, AAC, etc.? Will I be blunt, direct, indirect, etc. What will I say?
	Execute the plan	GO DO IT!
	Reflect on the interaction	How did it go? Did I get what I wanted? Did the other person react as I expected? Did they tell or show me how they felt or their thoughts?
	Problem Solve	If things didn't go as planned, how did I feel? Do I know how they felt? What can be changed?

Planning is Everything

Read the scenarios below. Pick the intent/s, the style you may use, and then plan out a message, or what you would say.

Your friend is telling you a story. You want to participate, but don't know the words they are using.

Intent:_____
Style:_____
Message:_____
_____
_____

Intent:_____
Style:_____
Message:_____
_____
_____

You saw a new movie over the weekend. Your classmates asked you how it was and what happened.

You are feeling bored at a party and would like to talk to some of the other guests.

Intent:_____
Style:_____
Message:_____
_____
_____

self-advocacy

Objectives:

- Identify areas of self-advocacy

- Sequence steps to self-advocacy

- Generate self-advocacy statements

- Identify my own needs

- Create self-advocacy visual

Self-Advocacy

Self-advocacy is communicating your needs in specific situations or environments. This can look like asking for help, communicating a difference, or asking for a tool. We can advocate for needs at school, at a job, with friends - just about anywhere! Things we may need to advocate for include:

Learning Supports

Communication Styles

Processing Needs

Sensory Needs

Basic Needs

Clarifications

Social Preferences

Emotional Regulation

Assistance

Let's Get Ready to Advocate!!!!

Advocating can feel uncomfortable sometimes. Being prepared can help us feel more comfortable. We can use these steps:

	Action	Questions to ask myself
	Identify what you are advocating for	What is it you need support with? What is the reason you need this support?
	Identify the support	What do you need for this scenario? Is it a tool, a strategy, an answer, etc.? Who may be able to help if you need it?
	Positive self-talk	Create a positive experience. "Everyone needs help." "I can do this." etc.
	Plan it out	What will I say? What communication style and modality will I use? Can I use one of these scripts? -"I (insert difficulty), so I need (insert tool/strategy)." -"I'm confused by (insert topic), can you help me?"

Stop! Advocate & Listen

Look at the pictures and decide what each person needs to advocate for. What will they say?

_____

_____

_____

_____

_____

_____

_____

_____

_____

_____

_____

_____

I Know Myself BEST

We have already learned that different brains mean different learning, communicating, and socializing.

Reflect on your preferred ways to listen:

 Sitting in chair

 Moving

 Using a fidget

 Repeating what I hear

 Sitting on floor

 Looking

 Looking away

 Eyes closed

Doodling

Something different:

_____

I Know Myself BEST pt. 2

Reflect on your preferred ways to communicate:

Eye contact

No eye contact

Small talk

Info dumping

Direct

Indirect

Blunt

Spoken language

Written language

AAC

Being still

While moving

Something different:

_____

I Know Myself BEST pt. 3

Reflect on your preferred ways to learn:

Reading

Listening

Discussions

A lot of info at once

Info broken down

Sitting near adult

Sitting away from adult

In a big class

In a small class

Sitting away from peers

Using a body double

Something different:
_____
_____
_____
_____

I Know Myself BEST pt. 4

Reflect on your preferred ways to regulate:

 Deep breaths

 Go for walk

 Meditate

 Time to myself

 Talk it out

 Use something heavy

 Listen to music

 Reduce noise

 Eat something

Something different:

I'm My Own Advocate

Before we can start advocating for ourselves, we need to know what we should advocate for, when we would advocate, and what we can say.

List 3 areas of need or differences you experience

1._____

2._____

3._____

When will you advocate for these needs?

1._____

2._____

3._____

What will you say for each need?

1._____

2._____

3._____

Advocate Anywhere!

It can be hard to advocate in the moment. When we are stressed, anxious, or experiencing other large emotions, sometimes our words fail us. Use the cards below to write out common self-advocacy phrases you may want to use. Cut it out, fold it in half, and put it in your wallet, backpack, purse, etc. You can laminate it (or use tape) to make it last longer. Plan it below:

Which 4 accommodations do you want to include?

_____

_____

_____

_____

_____

My Accommodations	Self-Advocacy Statements
• _____	• _____
• _____	• _____
• _____	• _____
• _____	• _____

What if I Don't Get What I Need?!

You've brainstormed ways to advocate for your needs, great job! Hopefully advocating for your differences and needs will make your life easier.

However, there may be some times that your needs are not accommodated. People may not understand the way someone else communicates, socializes, or processes the world around them. Here's things to do and remember:

- Restate you needs in a different way. Misunderstanding *do* happen.

- Reflect on if a different accommodation may be beneficial also.

- Recognize this relationship or environment may not be ideal for your needs.

- Remember that all brains work differently, and others are accepting of that. You will find accepting people.

- Use direct communication to communicate.

What is something you could say if you don't get what you need?

----

perspectives

Objectives:

- Define multiple perspectives
- Generate multiple perspectives
- Define communication breakdown
- Define Double Empathy Problem
- Reflect on breakdowns
- Generate own perspectives

Multiple Perspectives

Perspective taking allows us to determine what people may be thinking or feeling. During interactions, it is important to think about multiple perspectives. This includes our communication partner's AND our own perspective.

Thinking about multiple perspectives can help us understand breakdowns in interactions and problem solve. You can ask yourself questions to help decide the perspectives of everyone involved.

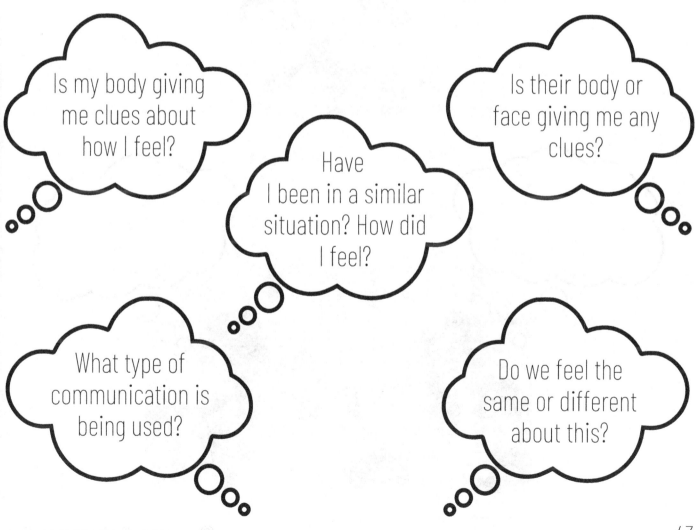

Is my body giving me clues about how I feel?

Is their body or face giving me any clues?

Have I been in a similar situation? How did I feel?

What type of communication is being used?

Do we feel the same or different about this?

Mind Reader

Look at the pictures below and guess what each person may be thinking or feeling.

Communication Breakdowns

When misunderstandings happen, it's a communication breakdown. This often occurs when people experience the world in different ways, maybe due to neurotype. This causes them to have different perspectives, communication, and social rules. These differences can make it difficult to put ourselves in someone else's shoes. We can call this the **Double Empathy Problem**.

Double Empathy Problem

The Double Empathy Problem explains that communication breakdowns are caused by both parties' misunderstandings, not just the fault of the neurodivergent individual.

Billy

Riley

For example: Billy (neurotypical) thinks Riley (Autistic) doesn't care about family dinner because they aren't making eye contact. Why may Riley not be making eye contact? How might Riley actually feel?

Communication Breakdowns

Reflect on a time you experienced a communication breakdown and/or the Double Empathy Problem. What were you thinking and feeling? What was your communication partner thinking?

Our Differences

Answer the questions about yourself below. Aside from your neurotype, your perspective can be shaped by past experiences, personal preferences, etc.

# of siblings: _____

Does your family get along? _____

Where did you grow up?_____

Guardian's job/s:_____

# of pets:_____

Favorite school subject:_____

Most important thing to me:_____

_____

Special interest/s: _____

_____

Something that drives me NUTS:_____

_____

Our Differences

Figure out someone else's experiences by having a conversation, doing research, or using what you already know about them. How are you the same or different?

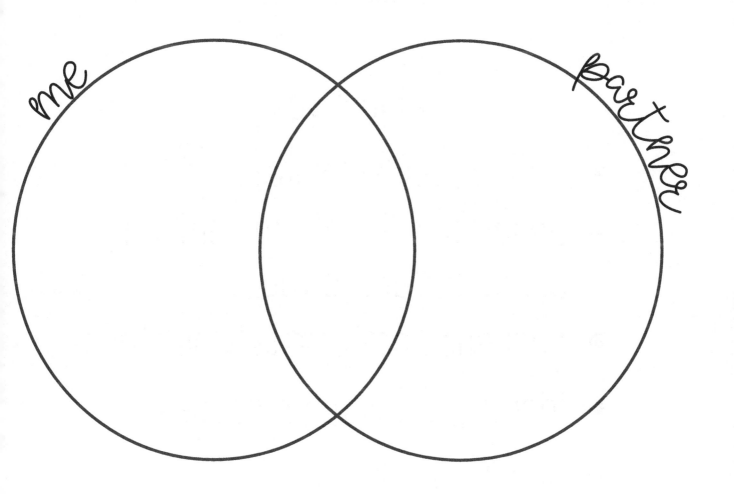

problem solving

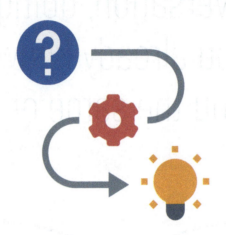

Objectives:

- Define problem solving
- Generate a list of problems that are important to you
- Sequence problem solving steps
- Identify problems & causes
- Generate solutions

Problem Solving

You will experience problems almost every day. It can range from spilling a cup of water, to getting lost, to having an argument with a friend. Problems that feel disastrous to one person may not bother another. Everyone feels differently about problems, and that's okay! No matter how we feel, we need to solve the problem. Some problems we can solve on our own, and others we may need help with.

Problem Solving

Rate each problem in terms of how it would make you feel! There are no right or wrong answers. Knowing which problems make us more upset or dysregulated can help us know how to solve it!

My Feelings

Don't really care   Getting anxious   This is huge

Unannounced schedule change

Argument with a friend

Lose a game

Get a bad grade

Problem Solving Steps

	Action	Questions to ask myself
⚠️	Identify problem	Is there a problem? What happened?
	Break it down	How/why did the problem happen? How do you feel about it? How do others feel about it?
	Self-advocacy	What do I need to solve the problem? Think about my basic needs, sensory needs, social/communication style. Will I need help? Who can help me?
	Brainstorm solutions	What is something that would help fix the problem? Can I think of any other solutions?
	Make a prediction	What could happen with each solution? What's something good about the solution? Is there anything bad? What am I hoping for?
	Pick your solution	Which solution is best? Which solution gets me what I want? Which solution helps me get what I need?

Solutions for 200, Alex!

Look at the pictures below.
Follow the problem solving steps for each picture.

Problem: _____

Cause: _____

_____

Perspective: _____

_____

Self-Advocacy: _____

_____

Solutions: _____

_____

_____

Prediction: _____

_____

Problem: _____

Cause: _____

_____

Perspective: _____

_____

Self-Advocacy: _____

_____

Solutions: _____

_____

_____

Prediction: _____

_____

Solutions for 200, Alex!
pt 2

Look at the pictures below.
Follow the problem solving steps for each picture.

Problem: _____

Cause: _____

_____

Perspective: _____

_____

Self-Advocacy: _____

_____

Solutions:_____

_____

_____

Prediction:_____

_____

Problem: _____

Cause: _____

_____

Perspective: _____

_____

Self-Advocacy: _____

_____

Solutions:_____

_____

_____

Prediction:_____

_____

Back to the Future

Thinking about past problems can help us think about the future. Knowing what worked, what didn't, how we felt, etc. can make solving similar problems easier. Reflect on each of these areas. What types of problems have you experienced? How would you solve the problem now?

Academic Problem: _____

_____

- Solution: _____

_____

Social Problem: _____

_____

- Solution: _____

_____

Vocational Problem: _____

_____

- Solution: _____

_____

Miscellaneous Problem: _____

_____

- Solution: _____

_____

relationships

Objectives:

- Identify types of socializing

- Identify own preferences

- Generate clues of friendship

- Identify ways to tolerate undesired pairings

Peer Relationships

The best part about communication is developing relationships with people. Everyone's idea of relationships (family, friends, romantic, etc.) is different. We want to find people we get along with. These people will have similar interests as us, respect our differences, desire the same interaction styles and frequency, and more.

If someone's views of a relationship doesn't align with yours, that's okay. They just may not be our ideal friend or partner.

In the picture below, what do you think their shared interest/s may be?

In Person, Social Media, & More

There is not just one way to socialize. We need to pick social scenarios in which we are most comfortable. Knowing our comfort level with different types of socializing, can help us find others who are similar. It can also help us know how to advocate for ourselves. Which of the following social interaction types are you most comfortable with?

In person

Texting

Phone calls

Social media

Video games

Video calls

Something different:

_____

Picture Perfect

Let's brainstorm!
What does your ideal social life look like?

Would you like more friends?   Yes   No

How many close friends would you like?_____

Do you want to hang out with friends?   Yes   No

How often would you like to hang out?_____

When would you like to hang out?_____

How would you like to hang out? (pick all that apply)
        in person   online gaming   virtually   something else

What personality traits would a friend have?_____

_____

Is it important that you have similar interests?   Yes   No

What do you like to do? _____

_____

What do you like to talk about? _____

_____

What activities would you like to do with friends? _____

_____

Ready... Set... Go!

We know who we want to be friends with! But, how do we know if someone wants to be friends with us? How can we let someone else know we want to be their friend? Some people may use direct communication to let us know. Some may not. This can cause confusion. Let's break it down. Describe your communication, and how others may communicate a desire to be friends, or not. Consider what may be said/not said, body language, facial expressions, etc.

	My Communication	Other's Communication
Want to be friends		
Does not want to be friends		

But... I Don't Like Them

Will you like everyone you meet? Will everyone you meet like you? The answer to both questions is no.
There is nothing wrong with that. Will you still have to interact with people you don't like? Unfortunately, yes.

We can use strategies to make these interactions easier and more tolerable.

- Monitor your feelings and energy
- Take a break
- Remember the time together is temporary
- Advocate for changes in groupings

What else can you do? _____

_____

If you are feeling uncomfortable with a grouping in class, at work, etc. what can we do?

What could you say? _____

_____

Who may be able to help? _____

_____

reflection

Objectives:

- Reflect on neurodiversity
- Assess your own learning

Reflection

Congratulations! You have completed
the Neurodiversity Workbook!

What's the most interesting thing you learned?_____

_____

_____

What do you think is most important?_____

_____

_____

Is there anything you didn't like? _____

_____

_____

Any questions? _____

_____

_____

Anything you'd like to know more about? _____

_____

_____

What I Know Now

Answer the questions below about what you learned regarding neurodiversity.

	Not so much	Kind of	Definitely
I know what the term neurodiversity means			
I know and can describe different neurotypes			
I know about my own neurotype			
I can name different communication styles			
I understand and utilize self-advocacy			
I understand the term multiple perspectives			
I know steps to solve problems			
I can identify what I look for in a friend or relationship			

Self-Reflection

This is a place to info-dump on what you've learned.

Instructional Notes

While using this resource, I challenge myself to be affirming in my practices and accept ALL forms of socialization and communication. Some tips that may help:

- Encourage self-reflection. This product is a guide and my hope is it will open discussions among you and your students

- Reflect on the Double Empathy Problem. This workbook targets skills to help build confidence, self-advocacy, and acceptance. Remember that there may be multiple answers to questions based on students' neurotypes.

- Teach autonomy, not masking. This product should empower students to live authentically, not blend in.

- Encourage students to explore what works best for THEM. This includes different types of social interactions. It's okay if your students prefer an online life (as long as it's safe). They will be able to find others who have this same preference.

- This workbook is not about right or wrong. It is to help students discover how they learn, communicate, and socialize best. After that discovery, how will they advocate for their ideal environments, educate others, and navigate a world that was created by neurotypicals, for neurotypicals?

While you can skip around to different sections, these lessons do build on one another. Skipping a section, may skip needed vocabulary for later skills.

Small Visuals

Cut out and laminate the visual sequences below as added support to supplemental activities, classroom visuals, etc. Larger versions are included within the workbook.

Problem Solving Steps

	Action	Questions to ask myself
⚠️	Identify problem	Is there a problem? What happened?
▣	Break it down	How/why did the problem happen? How do you feel about it? How do others feel about it?
📢	Self-advocacy	What do I need to solve the problem? Think about my basic needs, sensory needs, social/communication style. Will I need help? Who can help me?
💡	Brainstorm solutions	What is something that would help fix the problem? Can I think of any other solutions?
🔮	Make a prediction	What could happen with each solution? What's something good about the solution? Is there anything bad? What am I hoping for?
☝️	Pick your solution	Which solution is best? Which solution gets me what I want? Which solution helps me get what I need?

Effective Communication

	Action	Questions to ask myself
☝️	Pick intended message	What am I trying to communicate? What do I want? How do I want the other person to feel? What's my intent?
📝	Plan it out	Will I use spoken words, facial expressions, written words, AAC, etc.? Will I be blunt, direct, indirect, etc. What will I say?
✓	Execute the plan	GO DO IT!
💭	Reflect on the interaction	How did it go? Did I get what I wanted? Did the other person react as I expected? Did they tell or show me how they felt or their thoughts?
⚙️	Problem Solve	If things didn't go as planned, how did I feel? How did they feel? What can be changed?

Self-Advocacy

	Action	Questions to ask myself
💡	Identify what you are advocating for	What is it you need support with? What is the reason you need this support?
⚙️	Identify the support	What do you need for this scenario? Is it a tool, a strategy, an answer, etc.? Who may be able to help if you need it?
✂️	Positive self-talk	Create a positive experience. "Everyone needs help." "I can do this." etc.
📝	Plan it out	What will I say? What communication style & modality will I use? Can I use one of these scripts? -"I (insert difficulty), so I need (insert tool/strategy)." -"I'm confused by (insert topic), can you help me?"

Parent Questionnaire for _____

This school year we will be discussing neurodiversity. Neurodiversity refers to brain differences in learning, listening, communicating, socializing, and thinking. We can call the different brains, neurotypes. Neurodivergent brains work differently than how science expects. This includes Autism, ADHD, Anxiety, OCD, Dyslexia, Sensory Processing, Giftedness, etc. We would love for you to be involved in this learning process. Here are some questions to get us started.

Does your child know they have a disability?   Yes   No

If yes, how well do they understand their disability?   Not at all ←————→ Very well

If no, would you like them to know more?   Yes   No

What are your child's strengths? _____

_____

An important concept in our discussions at school will be discussing how our communication and socializing may be the same and different as our peers. We will discuss self-advocacy and problem solving for our needs. These concepts can be discussed without knowing our disability, but that information can help your child grasp a greater understanding.

Please indicate conversation topics you give permission for:

Disabilities in General   My Child's Disability   Strengths & Weaknesses

Individual Differences   Individual Needs   Self-Advocacy

Guardian signature: _____

Questions? Contact

Notes

Notes

About the Author

Katelyn is an ADHD SLP and strives to make affirming resources accessible to the education community. She is passionate about life skills, neurodiversity affirming practices, AAC, gestalt language, and functional communication.

Katelyn has been a Speech-Language Pathologist since 2015. She has experience with early childhood through transition aged students in schools and private practice.

In her free time, she loves sharing her SLP journey on Instagram (the_communication_classroom), hanging out with her family and friends, reading, and binge watching Netflix!

Katelyn's communication and social styles are reflective of her ADHD. She loves to info-dump about neurodiversity, AAC, and TikTok. She tends to interrupt when she's excited or passionate about a topic. Katelyn continues to work on connecting her "off topic" thoughts to the conversations so others can follow her train of thought. Katelyn benefits from using fidgets, sitting on the floor, and taking breaks.

Made in the USA
Monee, IL
02 March 2025

13217575R00044